cejc
10/19

D1209153

3-D ORIGAMI
PAPER BUILDING BLOCKS

RACHAEL L. THOMAS

Checkerboard Library

An Imprint of Abdo Publishing
abdobooks.com

Printed in the United States of America, North Mankato, Minnesota
052019
092019

 THIS BOOK CONTAINS
RECYCLED MATERIALS

Design: Christa Schneider, Mighty Media, Inc.
Production: Mighty Media, Inc.
Editor: Liz Salzmann
Cover Photographs: Mighty Media, Inc.
Interior Photographs: iStockphoto, pp. 6–7, 29; Mighty Media, Inc., pp. 1, 3, 4 (pattern), 8–27 (all), 28 (pattern), 30, 31, 32;
    Shutterstock Images, pp. 4–5, 5, 7, 28 (both)

Library of Congress Control Number: 2018966252

Publisher's Cataloging-in-Publication Data
Names: Thomas, Rachael L., author.
Title: 3-D origami: paper building blocks / by Rachael L. Thomas
Other title: Paper building blocks
Description: Minneapolis, Minnesota : Abdo Publishing, 2020 I Series: Cool paper art I Includes online
    resources and index.
Identifiers: ISBN 9781532119484 (lib. bdg.) I ISBN 9781532173943 (ebook)
Subjects: LCSH: Paper art--Juvenile literature. I Origami--Juvenile literature. I Japanese paper folding--
    Juvenile literature. I Paper folding (Handicraft)--Juvenile literature.
Classification: DDC 736.982--dc23

CONTENTS

GOLDEN VENTURE FOLDING

3-D origami is a special type of origami. In traditional origami, one sheet of paper is folded to create a model. In 3-D origami, many paper triangles are connected to create a model. These triangles are called units or **modules**. Modules **interlock** to create 3-D origami.

3-D origami is often called Golden Venture folding. This is because the Chinese **immigrants** who made 3-D origami popular traveled to the United States on a ship called the *Golden Venture*.

In 1993, the *Golden Venture* sailed from China to the United States with 286 men, women, and children aboard. These people wanted to enter the country illegally. However, the ship ran aground before it reached shore. Some of the Chinese immigrants died trying to escape. Others were arrested by US officials.

The surviving *Golden Venture* **immigrants** applied for political **asylum**. During this process, they were kept in prison. To pass the time, the immigrants made elaborate **3-D** origami models. The immigrants sold some of the models to raise money for legal fees. They gave other models as gifts to the people who helped them. The *Golden Venture* immigrants made 3-D origami popular in the United States!

MODULES

To make **3-D** origami models, you first have to make the paper **modules**. Origami paper is a good option for making modules because it is thin and easy to fold. But other materials could work well too. Some origami artists use materials such as old newspapers, magazines, and junk mail to avoid waste.

To make 3-D origami models, you'll need a lot of small paper rectangles. The length of each rectangle should be one and one-half times its width. For example, you could make them each 3 inches (7.5 cm) long and 2 inches (5 cm) wide.

Try stacking several sheets of paper and drawing the size rectangle you want on the top sheet. Then cut through all the sheets together to make several rectangles at once.

Making one **module** doesn't take long. But you'll need many of them to create most models. So be prepared to spend some time making modules. You could ask friends and family members to help so that the process goes more quickly. You can also buy packs of already folded modules online. This could save time, especially if you need enough modules to create large **3-D** origami models.

FOLD A MODULE

Here is how to make a **3-D** origami **module**. You will need many of these to create a 3-D origami model.

1

Place the rectangle on the table with a long edge at the top. Your module will be the color of the facedown side.

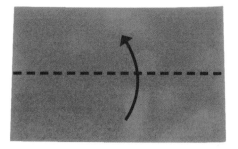

2

Valley fold the bottom edge to the top edge.

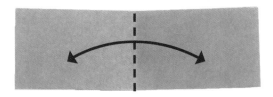

3

Valley fold the left edge to the right edge. Unfold.

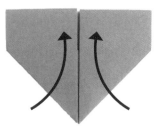

4

Valley fold the bottom edges to the center crease. Turn the paper over.

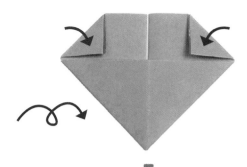

5
Valley fold the top corners
down into small triangles.

6
Valley fold the top edges
down toward the point.

7
Valley fold the left point to
the right point. Crease firmly.

Completed modules

COMMON FOLDING SYMBOLS

 Valley fold

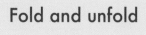 Fold and unfold

Turn over

CONNECTING MODULES

Here are some ways to connect **3-D** origami **modules**.

One-to-One Connection

Each origami module has two tabs and two pockets.

Connect modules by sliding the tabs of one module into the pockets of another.

Connecting modules one-to-one creates a single row.

Two-to-One Connections

Slide one tab from two **modules** into the pockets of a third module.

Slide the tabs of one module into the pockets of two modules.

Two-to-one connections can be used to create layers of modules.

TIPS & TRICKS

It can be tricky to keep modules in place. If the modules keep slipping out, put a very small blob of poster **putty** on each tab before sliding it into a pocket. This will hold the two modules together.

Do not use tape or glue. It is important that the modules be able to move around a little. This will let you push and pull your **3-D** origami model into its final shape.

11

FESTIVE WREATH

- at least
  30 modules

1

Arrange the **modules** in a row. Make sure they all face the same way.

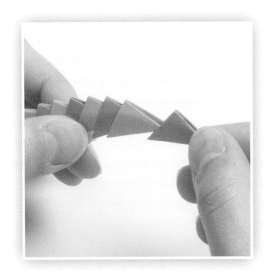

2

Connect the modules so they curve into a circle.

3

After all of the modules have been connected, bring the ends together and connect them.

TINY TREE

- **4 to 6 green modules**
- **brown paper**
- **scissors**

1

Cut a rectangle out of brown paper. It should be about the same size as the rectangles you used for the **modules**.

2

Place the rectangle on the table with a long edge at the top. Make a small fold in the bottom edge.

3

Continue folding the bottom edge until you have a thin strip of folded brown paper. This is the tree's trunk.

4

Fold the trunk in thirds.

5

Arrange the **modules** in a row. Alternate the direction they face.

6

Connect the modules in the order you arranged them.

7

Push one folded end of the trunk into the bottom module. Fold the other end of the trunk at a right angle. Use it to stand the tree up.

OUTRAGEOUS OCTOPUS

- 86 modules for the main body
- 2 darker modules for the cheeks
- 3 black modules for the eyes and mouth

1

Arrange 12 body **modules** in a circle. This is the first row of the octopus.

2

Use two-to-one connections to add a row of 12 body modules on top of the first (see page 11). You may want to use a little poster **putty** to keep these rows securely together (see Tips & Tricks on page 11).

3

Arrange ten body modules and the two cheek modules in a circle. There should be three body modules between the cheek modules. Connect a black module to the middle of these three body modules.

Continued on the next page.

4

Connect the **modules** from step 3 to the others to make a third row. Be sure to keep them in order.

5

Connect the remaining two black modules to the modules on each side of black module added in step 3.

6

Connect 12 more body modules to make a fourth row.

7

Connect 12 more body **modules** to make a fifth row.

8

Use eight body modules to make a sixth row. Connect each one over two or three tabs in the previous row (see page 11).

9

Connect the remaining eight body modules to the bottom row. The corner of each module opposite its points should stick out. These modules are the octopus's arms.

SILLY STRAWBERRY

- 59 red modules
- 7 green modules

1

Arrange 13 red **modules** in a circle. This is the first row of the strawberry.

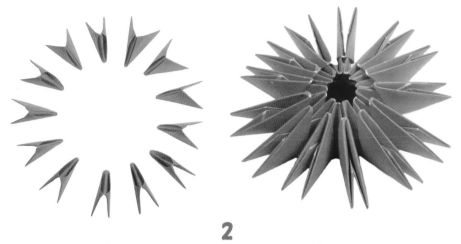

2

Use two-to-one connections to add a row of 13 red **modules** on top of the first (see page 11). You may want to use a little poster **putty** to keep these rows securely together (see Tips & Tricks on page 11).

3

Connect 13 more red modules to make a third row.

Continued on the next page.

4

Turn the three rows inside out. Be careful that the **modules** don't slide out of place.

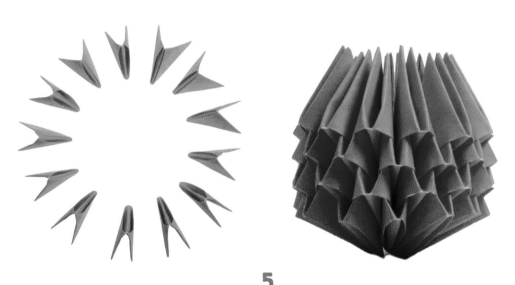

5

Hold the strawberry so the tabs of its modules point up. Connect another 13 red modules to these tabs to make a fourth row.

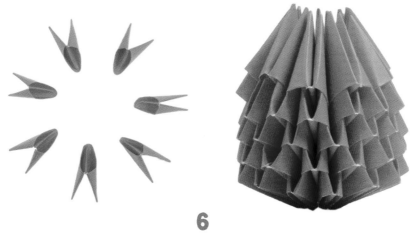

6

Use the final seven body **modules** to make a fifth row. Connect each one over two or three tabs in the previous row (see page 11).

7

Turn the strawberry over. Connect the green modules around the top of the strawberry. They should be spaced evenly. The corner of each module opposite its points should stick out. These are the strawberry's leaves.

CUTE CUPCAKE

- 48 modules for the cupcake
- 27 modules for the frosting
- craft glue
- red pom-pom

1

Arrange 16 cupcake **modules** in a circle. This is the first row of the cupcake.

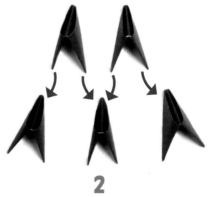

2

Use two-to-one connections to add a row of 16 cupcake modules on top of the first (see page 11). You may want to use a little poster **putty** to keep these rows securely together (see Tips & Tricks on page 11).

3

Connect 16 more cupcake modules to make a third row.

Continued on the next page.

4

Turn the three rows inside out.
Be careful that the **modules**
don't slide out of place.

5

Hold the cupcake so the tabs
of its modules point up.

6

Connect 16 frosting modules
around the top of the cupcake. The
corner of each module opposite its
points should stick out.

7

Use the final 11 frosting **modules** to make a second row of frosting. Connect each one over two or three tabs in the previous row (see page 11).

8

Glue the pop-pom to the top of the cupcake.

CONCLUSION

The art of Golden Venture folding has grown from being a political **statement** to something that anyone can try! Becoming a **3-D** origami artist takes practice. The more **modules** you make, the quicker and easier it will become. Repeat simple designs until you know them by heart. Then move on to bigger, more **complicated** 3-D models.

As you master the basics, don't forget to experiment with new designs. Mix and match colors and materials. Or add googly eyes, chenille stems and other decorations to bring your origami to life.

And like a true artist, keep your eyes and ears open for new inspiration. Have an adult help you find online videos of 3-D origami masters at work. Try some of their methods. One day, you could be the one showing your paper art to the world!

GLOSSARY

asylum – the protection given by a nation to someone who feels unsafe returning to his or her home country.

complicated – having elaborately combined parts.

immigrant – a person who enters another country to live.

interlock – to join or hook together.

module – one of a group of similar pieces that can be used together.

putty – a soft, moldable paste.

statement – an opinion or attitude that you express through your appearance and actions.

three-dimensional (3-D) – having length, width, and height and taking up space. "3-D" stands for three-dimensional.

ONLINE RESOURCES

To learn more about 3-D origami, please visit **abdobooklinks.com** or scan this QR code. These links are routinely monitored and updated to provide the most current information available.

INDEX